BIG&Little

by Marilyn Easton

SCHOLASTIC INC.

New York   Toronto   London   Auckland
Sydney   Mexico City   New Delhi   Hong Kong

Many people keep dogs as pets. One of the reasons dogs make great pets is because they are very smart. Dogs can learn tricks and protect their owners.

DOG

Puppies sleep a lot. A puppy needs about 15 to 20 hours of sleep each day. When they are awake, puppies are exploring the world around them, playing with toys, and chewing on everything. It's no wonder they need so much sleep!

Cats can be cute and cuddly. Sometimes a cat will let out an adorable meow if it wants attention. But if a cat hisses, it wants to be left alone.

CAT

Kittens play with yarn and other toys. They also like to sharpen their claws on scratching posts. Their claws can be sharp, so look out!

Horses have hooves at the bottom of their feet. The hard hooves protect their feet. Horse hooves are always growing, so they need to be trimmed—just like a fingernail!

HORSE

Baby horses are called foals. They have very long legs. A few hours after they are born, foals try to walk, but since their legs are so long they can have trouble keeping their balance.

FOAL

Cows are known for their milk, but male cows don't even make milk! Female cows are only able to make milk after they have had a baby. A heifer is a female cow that has not yet had a baby.

COW

When a baby cow, or calf, is born, it relies on its mom's milk. Newborn calves usually weigh between 50 to 100 pounds. Sometimes a cow can have twin calves.

CALF

Pigs have a reputation for being dirty. They may roll around in the mud, but it's only so they can keep cool. Pigs do not sweat, so they need to cool down somehow!

PIG

Baby pigs are called piglets. A mother pig gives birth to about 9 to 15 piglets at a time. That's a lot of piggies!

PIGLET

Ducks fly, walk, and swim. Their webbed feet help them paddle through the water. When they are out of the water, they use their one toe that is not webbed to help them walk.

DUCK

Baby ducks, or ducklings, are hatched from an egg. They poke their beaks against the shell. When the shell cracks, the duckling uses its beak to make the hole larger. Once it is big and strong enough, the duckling pushes its entire body out of its shell!

DUCKLING

Sheep are best known for their hair, called wool. Wool can be used to make a lot of things, including clothing. Once a sheep's wool is cut, it will grow back just like a haircut!

SHEEP

When baby sheep, or lambs, are four months old, they mostly eat grass. Lambs have eight teeth. Like humans, their baby teeth fall out and soon their adult teeth grow in.

LAMBS

Some lions live in groups called prides. Prides are mostly made up of female lions, with a few males. When lionesses hunt together, they have an easier time catching food. They can work as a team to trap their prey.

LION

Female lions take care of their cubs until they are about two years old. If the cub is female, she will stay with her mom. If the cub is male, he will be forced to leave the pride when he is about 3½ years old and he will have to live alone until he gets a pride of his own.

LION CUB

Giraffes have long necks. Their long necks help them reach their main food, the leaves of the acacia tree. Giraffes can extend their tongues around the sharp thorns on acacia trees, so they don't get pricked.

GIRAFFE

A baby giraffe, or calf, is sometimes left with a babysitter! Giraffe mothers will leave their calves together with other calves while they go off to find food for themselves. One female giraffe will stay behind and watch over the calves.

GIRAFFE CALF

The most special part of an elephant is its trunk. An elephant smells with its trunk. It also uses its trunk to spray itself with water to keep cool. An elephant can pick up objects with its trunk, too!

ELEPHANT

When a baby elephant, or calf, is born, it has a short trunk. As the calf grows, it starts learning how to use its trunk. Just like a baby human will suck its thumb, a baby elephant will suck its trunk, too!

ELEPHANT CALF

Chimpanzees live in areas that have a lot of trees, like rain forests. Chimpanzees swing from tree to tree to get around. When they are tired, they will take a nap in a tree.

CHIMPANZEE

Baby chimpanzees need their mothers for a longer time than most animals. Chimpanzee babies ride on their mothers' backs. Even after they start walking, the young chimpanzees will still stay with their mothers until they are about six years old.

BABY CHIMPANZEE

Pandas mostly eat a plant called bamboo. In fact, they like it so much that they eat about 80 pounds of it a day! Pandas need to eat a lot of bamboo to get enough nutrients.

PANDA

Baby pandas are very tiny when they are born. The mother panda protects her cub. But a mother's role is not always serious—baby pandas like playing with their mothers, too.

PANDA CUB

Polar bears live in the icy Arctic surrounded by freezing water. Their thick fur helps keep them warm. A polar bear's paws are rough, which keeps them from slipping when they walk on the ice.

POLAR BEAR

Polar bear mothers usually have twins. The mother and her cubs stay warm in their den during the winter. In the spring, they leave the den and the mother teaches her cubs how to find food.

POLAR BEAR CUB

Sea lions eat fish and other sea animals. When they swim in dark waters, sea lions can hunt using their whiskers. With their whiskers, sea lions can feel movement in nearby water. If a tasty fish swims close enough, the sea lion will know and then chomp down on its meal.

SEA LION

A baby sea lion, or pup, spends the first days of its life on land. Once it is a few weeks old, the pup can start swimming in the water. It must learn how to catch a fish, but it must also learn how to avoid being caught by the sharks that hunt them!

SEA LION PUP

Kangaroos have a great way of getting somewhere fast—they hop! They can travel pretty quickly by hopping. Larger kangaroos have been known to hop over 30 miles per hour. That's pretty impressive footwork!

KANGAROO

A baby kangaroo is called a joey. When it is born, it is not strong enough to survive on its own. The joey stays inside its mom's pouch, called a marsupium, until it is stronger. The joey peeks its head out of the pouch to see the outside world.

JOEY

Hippos are found in Africa. They spend a lot of time in lakes and rivers, and they can hold their breath underwater for five minutes or more. They move around in water by walking where it is not too deep. If a baby hippo, or calf, is born in the water, the mother will push her baby to the surface so it can breathe.

HIPPO and CALF

Whether it's a puppy or a lion cub, these baby animals and their families are totally cute! Even though they may look adorable, some of these animals are meant to be in the wild. For a friend to cuddle up to, try a kitten or puppy!